Plank by Plank

For Nina —
a fellow linguist
and adventurer!

Ted

Plank by Plank

Ted Higgs

THRP

The Heartland Review Press/Elizabethtown, KY

Elizabethtown
Community & Technical College

Printed in the USA

First Edition

ISBN

978-0-9996868-6-7

$14.95

Cover art: Photo by Ted Higgs

Printed by Ingram-Spark

In Memoriam

April Phelps Higgs
December 4, 1946-November 14, 2018

A Song for Miklós

Miklós Radnoti 1909-1944

Did you see the stars that night, or briars
dancing on the horizon beyond the camp?
For the Serb and Italian, Frenchman, Jew,
you sought a separate peace — all brothers,
mourning for homes that existed only
in dreams; not even the shadows were real,
nothing but your verses, plank by plank,
asking no forgiveness against the foamy sky
on their solitary nightly marches home.

The others clutched their hearts; you
clutched your poems, the last bitter spark.
Today you stand waiting for the answers
that never came, like a stunned angel,
patient in your forgiveness, your wooden
rest nestled among trees in Hosok park,
bronze shoes polished by youngsters
rushing past on the cobbled, stone path.

Shall we honor the dead? a young boy asks.
Perhaps it is he, I reply, standing here,
who honors us, but it is obvious the boy's
years early in his knowing, and I too late.

Table of Contents

A Song for Miklós   5

I.

Weaving the Dream   9
The Aerialist   10
Beyond the Statues   11
Palio di Siena   12
Feathers   13
Roping the Rhinoceros   14
The Typesetter's Song   15
A Song for Melisande   16
The Appointment   17
Venezia   18
Museum Solitaire   19
The Cat on the Balcony   20
Artichokes   21
Songbird   22
The Reading   23
Painting the Leopard   24
Fumo   25
A View from the Window   26
Judging a Pencil Sketch   27
The Chorus at Picasso's   28

II.

On the Locale   30
Paraskevi   31
The Island   32
A Hawk in the Greek Hills   33
The Silence   34
The Coming of Spring   35
Aurora   36
Pizzica, the Spider's Dance   37

Tino's Chandeliers   38
Landlines   39
The Passing of the Billy-Boy   40
Riding South from the Y   41
A Window on the Bay   42
Requiem   43
To M.   44
The Door   45
Night Thoughts on Athos   46
The Artist's Death   47
Road Adagio   48
Woman with a String   49

III.

The Barrette   51
Hokkaido in the 50's   52
Gallery Space   53
Bella Napoli   54
Game Day   55
Luca at Play   56
Gracie's Pulpit   57-8
Girl Running   59
Greek Dolls   60
Hymettos   61
The Painter Going Blind   62
Train Sounds at a Distance   63
Little Johnnie, Auditor   64
The Passing of Edward Schwarz   65-6
The Arena   67
The Myrtle Hour   68
Summer Sketches   69
Pictures in the Attic   70
A Final Parting   71

Notes   74-5

I.

Weaving the Dream

I imagine you sitting at Chaucer's *lome*,
the tiny crosses rising and falling
at your hand's command—
the gradual diminishing of space.
I imagine your creation complete,
or nearly so,
our poems shunting back and forth,
templed by our thumbs in folding—
our hands so often cupped
in each other's, my thoughts
picking their way through.

You raise your head to object,
but the heddles plunge unalterably down,
and with the shedding
the gradual awakening of desire,
a thread soon beaten into the weave.

Now only the supernatural remains.

Perhaps this is what you feared
would change, this other, unknown
until the end.
But one senses a beauty, nonetheless,
unfolding, a confidence
that the final creation bears pursuing,
that the final trust is worth the making.

The Aerialist

The old aerialist, drunk with his joy for the ropes
knowing this must surely be his last walk
has stepped out anyway, defying all odds.
Perhaps to rage against the dying of this love
he comes bringing his high theatrics, turning
side to side, waiting for that whisper
he shall never hear again, as he inches forward,
feeling anew the pulse of the wire — as once
putting his ear to the track he sensed the train —
and imagines this message in the dying electricity
of his mercurial path a call, a shift of heart,
a return, but the tightrope calms, the moment passes,
and he turns his eyes to the distance ahead
knowing finally that one uncertain step
could win him closure, sending him into the netless
darkness of the years gaping ever before him
in that solitude he has chosen above all save one,
and here above the others, above the cheers
and jeers he so artfully avoided for so long, flying
high above their blurred faces, exactly here
he must decide — to walk the empty rope
until its farthest end or end it quickly
surrendering himself thus to the greedy pull
of the ignorant, yet hungry, merciless crowd below.

Beyond the Statues

for Seferis

Somehow the sea demands its revenge on us all.
This thought you carried lightly as an oar
into the mountains.
The times were unpropitious, the wars,
the sad legions cast into the desert.

Don't talk to me of ships,
nightbirds in the harbor, the taverns of youth
bright with the sun's weave,
natives who frown and draw back from strangers.
Don't talk to me of solitude,
you who have returned with half-closed eyes.

Only this road and the sky exist, only this sign
broken in the dust, an ancient story
whispered in tavernas.

It had been years since I had heard the sea
the memory darkening like a cloud,
the wind sweeping past the bar
as each time we set our oars the sea responded.
After three days we sighted land,
three days of darkness; but it was illusion.
We set to anyway, beached on ice.

The old ship on the ice among the birds
coming to meet us, hundreds standing
in the silence as we drank our wine
and stared into the dark eyes of comrades,
the wind whirling round as our eyes
closed, our heads dropt, and we slept.

What they don't know, the storytellers,
is that death always comes from the sea:
arrivals and abandonments, a temple of sand
built on the ashes of generations.

Palio di Siena

One comes expecting silent hooves,
a brush of color caught
from the corner of one's eye,
a modern awareness
of the spirit of the place,

But nothing happens in the square,
the waist-high markers
arrange themselves in uncomfortable,
muted intervals, a boundary

Of vendors, the shadow of the tower
cutting their ranks
drawing one's attention to the passage
of time and the flags that change

To scarves, like the brunettes
dancing beneath the tower,
an indistinguishable minagerie.

One comes expecting color, disordered
rows, a hundred fantasies
painted across the dusty square
empty of the dreams one comes expecting.

Feathers

A man walks down the aisle selling pillows;
pillows with feathers, he insists, as the bus awaits
its departure to Vegas, the promised land,
the late-night station a shelter, the insobrients
settling in, bible sellers, prostitutes, homeless,
pilgrims all, on their way to their fortunes.
Beside me an old drunk has fallen asleep
smoking, the ash drooping ready to fall,
his bag of bottles rattling as he shifts his feet.
And finally the driver climbs on, grabbing
the handle, shutting the coach door as though
sealing a coffin on its way to the furnace.
And slowly the lights of town flow softly past
like waves chasing a caique on the Aegean,
the bus finding its metered pace, heading north
onto the desert, a sparse dawn breaking,
a collage of cacti and rabbits and tumbleweed.
At journey's end we start our slow descent
to try once again the odds, driven by desires
that flicker in the wind and vanish, a faint
whisper of a kiss heard in the heart, a mirage
of sound snuffed even as we expectantly arrive.

Roping the Rhinoceros

The woods stand before us like a veil
verdant in its menacing, and outside time.
Only the slight swaying of the grass
betrays his presence just beyond the tree line,
so we wait, breath held over hearts
pounding, the thumping grown louder,
our lassoes coiled in anticipation,
an ambush misplaced from the old west,
the cool wind blowing, bringing into form
the leather scent, the tattoo of its footfalls,
and I imagine Bradamante riding her steed
forward into combat, her golden thighs
fast against flanks, galloping in rippled
harmony, or lying in long fresh grass,
hands stretched toward the turquoise sky,
her white shield and plume tossed aside,
until the crash of forest birch brings us back,
the heat like napalm exploding around us
and suddenly he's there, racing to free
himself, sensing the danger as we rise ghostlike
from our trench to cast our lariats,
like guy wires tossed onto ancient quays
hoping for purchase, and the rope springs taut,
the horn swinging in axlike precision,
legs swimming thickly in the stirred
dust of evening, and then silence,
as we remain poised, not yet ready,
the only sound the beast's measured
breathing reminding us of our conquest,
a first time like no other, or nearly so.

The Typesetter's Song

I run my fingers over the braille of the type,
the ink cool to the touch, and the words sing
from the page. The tray, a platen of delicate prose,
sits waiting for the press of paper and the coil,
the gentle torque starting its slow descent.
I stand patient in anticipation, rubbing
the dye between fingers, like the juice of fruit
wiped from one's chin after the first bite
or the moisture from the lips of a lover,
the piquant taste leaching through, the inked
tray now making contact, the inkers
like castanets fixing the tempo, the image
taking shape on this broad canvas of print.
There's something about this give and take,
like rowing on a lake in the twilight,
leaning into the motion and sliding back
chest and shoulders pulled tight again and again,
the breathing syncopated, the eyes open or shut,
the sudden splash of oars when one's rhythm
goes awry, our modest craft gone aground.
Just so one awaits the finished page, quartered,
bound, and finally cut, the gentle reader
slicing the virgin fold, moving quire by quire
along the inked intaglio, until the end,
the last whispered syllable captured,
a mysterious translation of sound and sense,
meaning, type, space, timing, and desire.

A Song for Melisande

Que les anges nous pardonnent

You look down with half-closed eyes,
half perceiving innocence, balanced still
in the round glass of a passing moment.

Here your lips, the perfect center,
perfect you: your hair dense
darkness falling, a lovely
mystery lightly in the night.

From your fingertips the water
trembles and glides
ringlets that expand and expand again.
No one is present to see these
reflections: hair mirroring darkness
mirroring night sky.

Lightly your fingers touch you,
hold you in meditation:
the broken fragments redefine themselves
in the glass of possibility.

Together, yes, for this split moment; yours
is the only face, and yours
alone the eyes that look so deeply
into time.

In the night the water
trembles knowingly, and the stars
in your darkened heaven
go out one by one
erasing the blanched petalous flower
of your being, and still
you continue there unmoving, waiting.

The Appointment

Today a thousand pigeons have flown by
casting angry glances her way
as though she were out of place in her unmoving,
the young woman sitting by the fountain,
handsomely expectant,
a thousand, thousand possibilities;

I imagine her every move,
every change as she rises,
the handshake that doesn't quite end,
her nervousness, a friendship
like a small bird
that passes into the flow of the air.

And here you are, quietly composed
on this wooden bench, listening to my poems
watching the fountain as I once watched
the moon rise over the river,
the shadows of the dead
dancing like pigeons over stones
smooth with a thousand hopes, all confused.

Yet there is a spell that wants saving,
a mystery that pulls
each to the darkness of the other.

So here you are, an unfamiliarity
one meets like a child
that sleeps in stations waiting
for a train that never comes
or dying men chanting ancient songs
in lost dialects.

So here you are, lovely in your perplexity,
waiting.

Venezia

Only when the larger boats go by
does the water reach me, sitting now
drinking wine in late afternoon.
Nearby a tourist boat crosses a crusty
intersection, followed by a funeral
moving northward, the first boat
carrying its cargo, and a merchant
winding his watery way home, waving
as his fruit stand drifts slowly by.
Today, another transit, a farewell,
an artist staying behind, living a dream
more imagined than real, painting;
it's her intensity I remember, eyes
that would dart from subject to canvas
and back, like a bee between flowers,
the nights together under the stars,
that faint trace of us, a sketch drawn
upon this caesura of time, a canvas
where memory, that final anodyne,
leaves its measured vestiges before it too
must fade into the canal's darkness.

Museum Solitaire

How softly the blue snow melts, the branches
unfolding, the eye sweeping lightly
side to side like the brush strokes of Cezanne,
and I know what it means
to feel sadness for such blues, melancholy
for the leaving of simple things:
the green bananas and flags of Chirico,
his figures, their shadows bigger than themselves.

Why do they pull me so? Their haunting nature,
perhaps, like the solitary figure
disappearing beneath Feininger's viaduct
or Ernst's blind swimmer, but perhaps this
is what one is meant to see, the stone
Miró threw that will never hit the bird.

I stand watching Seurat's petit points explode,
three clouds floating dreamlike on canvas,
a suspension more of petals
than cloud, the sea breaks splitting
the sand and music that laps
at the shore like waves,
the music of Rousseau's dream,
the dark figure, mysterious and unexpected:
images that burst into the gallery
into me, so personal
I fear to name them lest they fly.

The Cat on the Balcony

When Luca rises to the sun's rays
peeking through the window, she grabs
her storybook and heads outside
to her balcony, graying in the morning
light, the cat sleeping as always
in the pot absent of flowers, to talk,
to tell her stories heard last at bedtime.
What the cat understands we may
never know, but her purr suggests
she gets the sense of what Luca pretends
to read to her as the sun lifts
over the tiled roof, and the noise
of Budapest once more drowns out
the dreams of the young girl
who has placed herself and the cat
in the story she tells, little knowing
that she has become that star that sweeps
across this narrative space invisible
except in fleeting moments of imagining,
a liberation one hopes will never fade.

Artichokes

Why must one pay for artichokes
over and over, for objects in the world, images
of experience, things?

How would you sketch this need, exploring the world
as you do with pencil and brush?
Is it so simple? To sketch the inexplicable,
to paint what lies within us:
images that pull others in their wake, exquisitely.

A still life of a thistle, perhaps,
the customary pricks worn smooth
with evolving
like creativity or desire
the sharp edge maintained with difficulty;

Or yourself, perhaps,
sitting in Venice near the water,
the failing sun combing its golden fingers
through your hair.

Or two people among strangers,
eating artichokes, knowing
such fruits offer themselves to consciousness
always too late, as one leaves:
memories, half remembered, half felt,
a new friend, a fellow artist, left too soon.

Songbird

Outside my window a songbird sings
discovering himself in sound. His voice careens
through trees to the open air and hills;
invisibly he soars high in his ecstasy
as rain sweeps down surrounding the berries,
the sweet fruit hanging still
in the breeze that ripples, recalling

perhaps some Aeolian ode, a joy
that beetles above branches in the rain,
droplets sliding down like the anxious hands
of lovers that glide in stolen moments
along the landscape of desire,
my mirrored movement an image
present in darkening silence, turning

outward in the widening gyre, moving
from branch to bough beyond, as spirits might,
leaping from petal to petal softly
until the dawn and the still now of present time,
as he remembers his voice and calls
his distant mate to wake from her dream,
his deep, full plaintive call echoing
once and once again and then no more.

The Reading

This morning I am reading about desire
holding as I do a stone, a petrified rock —
yet no rock at all, but wood, a living form,
once alive, like emotion, now dormant
but undeniably real — and so I read on,
its multi-faceted, vitrescent face catching
the light at all angles, its milky, rusty
quartz held in the creases of my palm.

As I read, remembering the passion, the tree
blossoms anew, annulling its weathered age,
the silent force of anticipation so real
and the sadness quiet as this mute wood
held tightly as I read awaiting her coming.

Painting the Leopard

Once your leopard's in position, it's time
to check out your equipment.
First, make sure that the brush is sturdy,
all the bristles clean and erect,
make sure the tip is moistened ever so
slightly with paint;

Then you may begin, but slowly,
moving the brush to the leopard's first
spot, working it evenly back
and forth, just there; you'll notice some
effect of this initial brushing,
a soft soothe, a purr perhaps, and fur
that warms to your strokes.

Paint there for a while, and then
move on, applying bolder strokes, further
along. By now you will have lost
all conception of spots, per se,
having discovered contours and crevices
much more conducive to such painting;

You'll notice, too, some effect of this
secondary stroking, for the leopard will grow
excited and volatile, but don't despair,
such response is healthy,
and you'll emerge, both well tempered,

The leopard freshly painted, and you,
satisfied to know the task well worth
the preparation, precision and care,
your first beautifully painted leopard,
panting and happy.

Shall we meet in Buda, or there beyond the river,
in the park, when the smoke clears and the dreaming
stops, the floating islands dock, and the wild cormorants
circle, dip, and are gone back to their source?
Long before such disappearances, in that split
second when the dew leaves the petal and drops
and the morning sun glances from its side, in its prismatic
moment there will gleam forth from within a voiceless
beam of hope carried on its irrevocable path down-
ward, unnoticed till it too hits the ground, and then
the silence will rise to consume that space, opening out
beyond the verge, fixing itself in time, static
in the eternal moment of its final tacit crescendo.

A View from the Window

Den Haag, the Netherlands

Between the real and its opposite, a shore,
as here, not quite metaphor, but
from my room I catch a glimpse, where
land dares touch the sea, watching
the waves wash up on the unwritten sand.
To the left, a brick wall, a spiral stair,
a triptych of naves along the façade.
Beyond, the lights of the ships blink
below the horizon, an imaged semaphore
arriving from beyond the bar, skimming
across the surface like the stones we tossed
as kids skittering across the water
once, twice, and a third before sinking.
From below, the evening sounds
like those of campfires crackling
with reflection, the lights of the city
prismed in the gentle rain, a kaleidoscope
whose slight twist effects new worlds,
as here, hearing the surf, watching
it write its song upon the opposing shore,
unnoticed by the crowd who scurry
in their myrmidon ways to an end
they believe they know beyond doubt
as the tattoo continues on the beaten shore.

Judging a Pencil Sketch

Of course this has the qualities
one needs in such a sketch
just as it stands.
The cage, the central image,
set in stark, but clear,
contrast to the canary,
but you should perhaps
erase the bird and put yourself —
No — better place mankind
behind the bars, persuasively.

Drop them deep in concrete
sleep, stroking hard. Sharpen
your finest pencil
for your disfigurement,
and with a hand much lighter,
draw obscenely on the wall,
the window and the floor
just out of view,
perfection intended.

Then let the art eraser devour all —
after which, you're done.
And what remains will be
a memory, a vagueness of space.

From this expression art will smile,
awaiting another's purer
translation of the real.
Except for these conditions,
I approve.

The Chorus at Picasso's

for Mick

Empieza el llanto/de la guitarra.
Es inutil/callarla.
— Lorca

Sometimes what seems slow is not — the burning
fuse snaking to its charge — and Picasso's,
the mood one felt arriving there, the spark
almost visible, the charming new poems
and old — Vergil, who would have thought, a voice
like that of Dido's sister Anne rising
from the page — our host a modern rhapsode,
a seasoned bard revealing in his song
words that scored our hearts, recalled even now.

It wasn't the night, the mantic musings,
the poetry like sweet Mareotic wine.
Horace would have seized his lyre and joined us,
bringing down his bow, taking back his vow
to leave the field, giving himself again
to the call of beauty, or Orpheus
watching the ancient giants as they slowed
at their tasks to his song, or Picasso
painting the sad guitarist whose slow notes
enthralled us, a richness like honey poured
at evening, as we watch Selene rise,
her moistened fingers touching us, as we
rejoin the chorus dancing in the halls
of time, and friends whose mellic voices still
gather me to them, in their own slow time.

II.

On the Locale

Here the train begins to slide past images
perhaps too easily recalled, past doorways
static in the flow of time, past lovers
locked in each other's arms, past a young woman
standing faintly visible, as though a memory
as sweet as wine, and as rare
on my recent lips, moving now forward
to shake clinched fists at the coming dawn,
daring the sun to rise from the gathered darkness.

Here pockets of time stretch, scattered
along the tracks like poems fallen
through my mind, half composed,
as the train moves forward slowly,
tentatively into landscape just now
being sculpted by our hearts.

Here in your eyes one reads promise,
inspiring and inspired, changing everything
they touch, intimating something yet to come —
if only in my insistent interpreting —
a tenderness impossible to hide, impossible.

And on that thought the train jolts forward
anxious to depart, leaving all patterned images
behind — doorways, lovers, others, all
earlier destinations, real or imagined —
moving instead into this new terra carrying
not a few ghosts from both sides, and yet
somehow distinctly ours, precious and forever.

Paraskevi

Friday will always be a day of preparation,
drawn unfettered by the weekend's allure,
as we would find, watching the purpling sky,
the Eta Aquarid meteors, their sudden spark,
a brightness waiting just beyond our vision
to surprise us before fading into the invisible.
You had been writing, conjuring *mots justes*
like swans to gather above the page, to wheel
suddenly into a cloud of ghostly meaning,
yet such symbols need time to build, to crest
spontaneously, thus writing and our lives,
two sides of a sheet pulled taut between us.
Come, I whisper, entering your reverie,
and you turn, your pensive pen held still
like a baton poised, an aria just beginning,
chanson d'amour, a paean to Freyja, heard
across the darkening lake, where dragonflies
glide above the mirrored meteoric deep,
an effluviance caught just above the wave.

The Island

If there be poetry, it's there
in the soft subtleties of your body, resting
hot upon the sand and my breathless
desires spread leaf thin, thrown
onto the sea like trawling nets,
hoping to catch some purchase
beneath the waves of your reverie

As now looking down into your eyes,
I see sky, the sun's reflection
and myself floating there,
a cloud over the beautiful
terraces and ravines of your geography
that lure me like a lost explorer
far from home, who finds
all unexpected, hills and hollows
long forgotten, ancient stores of pressed honey,
still sweet to the tongue's touch.

And in these moments before the first
kiss, the first soft exploring
touches of kindness, friendship, longing,
pleasure, I hold my breath that there be
no flight nor escape,
nor ship captained away,
and our island floating free
above all other islands and worlds, real
or imagined, just we two, together.

A Hawk in the Greek Hills

Springing high from the peak, wings spread wide
over the shadows, he catches the sun
and glides

past the stadium, by the bodies
of men carved into stone and the others, their spectral
substance still in shade;

past the theatre, the mind's shell
cupped like a human hand, the fingers raised,
its marble center, the chorus moving
forever backward against a scene worn smooth;

past the temple, deeper still, unaltering
the spirit's monument to itself, its tablets
bearing their fiery emblems into time;

flash left, wings down canyon and the caves,
tripods abandoned, fissures closed;
past the final ruins
unidentified in the unfolding, precariously
balanced on the edge; and finally
dives,

all else a prelude and pause, down
into empty space and free,
and in that instant of separation
his eye catches the boats, the coast and the sea,
the green expanse,
the crags, the laurels, and finally
silence.

The Silence

In high places the consecrated statues stand
like monks, their shoulders piercing heaven;
here before vespers the moon rises early,
capturing a gull lost on its way to the sea;
and here the full breasted woman waits
before climbing to hang handkerchiefs
on the moon; and here ancient Ajax turns,
reluctant to care, as we might, leaving a friend.

It's the unknowing, the making sense of things.
It's like dancing with a giant bear, awkwardly,
laughing and twisting, the fur wet, his claws
tapping a wild tattoo on the boards,
or like steering a large canoe down river
and nothing to guide it along but a pole
that you keep pushing and pushing
into the fine mud as though grounding
your bitterness just there in the soft loam
of deepening memory; or beautiful Dido turning
from her weakness, returning to the forest
too late, too late in the losing of partners
safely buried now in the dunghill of dreams.

And here I sit in Saint John's cave, and hear
the years as they wash up in the surf,
beyond the armies of tourists, crusaders,
and saints come to Patmos to breath
its holiness, drowning in a confusion of babel,
and the rock ledge just there where his scribe
set down his dreams, as he gazed
into his fissured ceiling, cracks torn
in his imagined world, as its vestige escaped
into scribal hand, and he remained silent
in a world silent to his knowing.

The Coming of Spring

Like the smoke of mountain stoves untended,
my thoughts fill the quiet room;
outside the swirling wind knocks sharply
on windows double-shuttered
against the spring.

Beyond, the mountain peaks
like young breasts rise tenderly
into the flaming air
where angels hang still with hidden knowledge.

Here the sad lover sings
to women as they pass, their sweet perfumes
smelling strangely of decay,
birds that bank and fall,
drowning themselves in shadows.

And here the starling frozen near the stream
awakens and darts past my window
as the lover's notes fade
slowly down the valley.

Soon the day's carefree meltings cease,
and all returns to stillness.
Neither winter nor spring is hard,
only the silent change,
the shifting shadows
that race across the valley floor in evening.

Aurora

die Dämmerung . . . man weiß sein Tiefe nicht –
aber man fühlt sie.
– Elsa Bernstein

Softly the dawn drifts through the hall,
taking its slow time to arrive, as though

hesitant to leave, wishing to cling,
surrounding you there in silhouette,

a late Pre-Raphaelite image, turned
just so, but the wave breaks finally

rushing past, and you turn as though
hearing something unheard by others

and rise now reciting German poetry
about nightingales and lovers, love
among the ruins, as twilight approaches.

Pizzica, the Spider's Dance

She lies stock-still as the music starts,
her white dress hanging limp, a sheet thrown
over the hard floor, the ancient *masseria* dirt
pounded smooth over time, tambourine
and drum, the violin following, pacing her throes,
faux lovers three, and her sister by the fire,
in her lap an icon of St. Paul, its golden face
aged by ancient smoke spiralling along the walls,
the sharp nettling sound of the crackling log,
a whip prodding the tarantine tempo forward,
and the music touches her, a ruby red *salice*
splashed on the incandescence surrounding her,
the wolf spider's venom spreading slowly,
a common bond, a need felt in the blood,
and she rises, dancing across the dirt floor,
her slippers like dolphins skimming the waves,
and from the whiteness her true lover appears
joining her in the moist Pugliese heat, and she
feels his presence, a white cloud of sound,
his breath a shadow haunting the grove, recalling
the olive tree's hard fruit rippening in the sun,
and they embracing in its shade, quiescent
in the land's mad obscure, the inquiet cicadas,
the hidden honey of the hives, a finger pricked
picking berries, his voice like the roar of the sea,
and the intimate light of the moon, the resin taste
of his body on the beach, their fire on the rocks,
ghostly silhouettes moving on sea-washed stone,
her dulcet body dampened in the salt spray,
and she beats time to the insistent tambourine
tapping out its metronomic call while her shadow
dances beside her, steps as old as the land,
the hillside town, her small hut, this threshing floor,
her tread on the dead earth, a sigh escaping,
and the sound of the violin and the music
of her cries, *ahii*, escape on the wind
to wash over the hills, through the olives
and grapes, past the church, the abandoned
hearths, the splashing sea foam of the surf,
as the drum's final tap sounds, the violin's bow
makes its last pass, and all returns to silence
and the twilight sounds of evening once again.

Tino's Chandeliers

The trip was always mysterious, slipping
beyond the icons, the glittering mosaics,
moving northward, to Murano and its glass
leaving behind the antique chapels, gondaliers
drinking their coffees at dockside, north
to Tino's just across the last bridge, the path
a moss encrusted *calle* on a dark canal.
Entering I always sensed the magic,
the heat from a crowded vitreous sky —
suspended crystal reliques just beyond
one's reach — as I searched each orb for clues,
stories locked in their luminescence:
a youth combing the waves from boatside,
the wine-dark hair of an absent love; a man
spread-eagled on ice looking into the darkness;
a crone crimson-draped, slowly luminous,
offering an object in ardent flame,
and I not daring to name this gift remain
adrift, dreaming once again of scarlet suns,
glass beads, like the marbles of my youth
shot from the circle in the dirt, leaving
to chance whatever might come at last
knocked loose from the center, images
rising to the surface, polished memories,
the floats of ancient fishing nets washed
finally onto the vagrant shore of memory.

Landlines

Tonight a thousand voices whisper
along telephone wires stretched taut
as though by wooden giants across fields,
and I have heard them buzzing
like cacadas, or the myriad vultures
that range along them waiting to seize
their prey, like musicians searching
for a quarter note one has missed
somehow slipping off the scale.
Now all that's left is this faint buzz
under their vague shadows as I wait
for answers not yet heard that I know
will someday come along these lines
that stretch like a hand pointing forward
to a future where there will be answers,
passing through the forests of the night.

The Passing of the Billy-Boy

From the middle distance mist the billy-boy
sails in slow pace forward towards us
on the bridge's height, awaiting the passage

as thirty years before we watched the barge
slip past, the weathered nereid carved
on her mast still visible, her auburn hair

like ropes coiling around her waist, bowing
forward saluting the well-wishers topside
as the ship passes beneath, the sailors

moving upon the deck, charmed voyagers
chasing their cherrywood dreams, waiting
at the capstan to lower the mast, her hair

in auburn waves floating, as the barge slues
starboard and the sailors snap from reveries,
the ropes and windlass taut as they pass,

translating her phantom shade to rise afresh,
her traverse complete, on the other side,
rising as though to answer questions forgotten,

memories that stand like spectres, silently
on sand awaiting passage, the nymph
her glossy eyes aglitter with her salty tears,

and deep within one feels a mounting sigh,
a pounding heart waiting to break free.

Riding South from the Y

We leave the reading and find the subway,
south through Manhattan to South Ferry.
Unnoticed we slip past the park
fresh snow hanging from trees, the lake frozen.
Down the car a young girl sings to herself
in Spanish, a Christmas carol, as though
offering absolution, repeating the same verses
to the dark air, to the glass, to the chorus
of silent faces, to the deaf man with the cards;
this dark angel, her reflection, lozenges
of flashing lights and pitch darkness.
We cross the theater district imagining
the dramas happening above, the Square,
heading once again into the maelstrom
of night, passing below the known, a buried
temporal flux, sweeping past unobserved
to NYU, the Village, and Saint Mark's,
the Poetry Project, a chorus of voices
echoing in the void, a creative pulse
launched across time, and track's end,
the wharf and waiting ferries, their red bulbs
a cipher awaiting translation, an enigma met
as we steer south to the dock and final repose.

A Window on the Bay

Today as the white-tailed gulls sheer
past my eastward window
I hear the waves hammering the shore
and in the growing darkness see
that compassionate stranger, a shade
that pulls everything back like nets —
quite fortunately, I suppose —
from the undefined, defined sea.

Without glasses in this 3-D world
I watch an artist apply his colors
after the base coat has dried, his notes
after the music sets, his abstract theme
allegro (you might say), ma non troppo,
the casual warning of a friend
echoing like the opening, astonishing awe
of a church — the angels in meisin glass
or stained — closed for reparations,
the spirit gone.

On the nearby shore, past the gulls,
the island's single commuter scuds
furiously homeward, closing a meditation
on the sea's wintry, raspy voice.

Requiem

The rolling thunder settles in, running
over the mountains, and the darkening
shade spools across the limpid wood;
despair like a heavy haze wraps 'round us,
a blanket from which we must unscroll
ourselves, yet there is something to be gained
riding this wave, catching the rolling surf
as it hurls us forward towards a shore
that retreats forever as we in desperate
approach, dumb to the sound of the waves,
hear only the deadline of lost connection.

Shall we compose the music now, a ballade
to be learned by students, from memory,
sung to a Joni Mitchell melody, something
about clouds and illusions, and giving
yourself to a cause that remains a dream,
the fantasy of overwrought imagination?

The solace, such as it is, the future
remains comfortably inscrutable now,
like the fig tree, thought dead, bursting with life,
nature restoring itself as always
despite the best irrational attempts
to commute the goodness that here abounds.

To M.

I wanted to write a poem for you
now, this year, a magical poem, a flower
whose petals years from now would open
to surprise you, as they may now.

It's funny how everything keeps running
back to age and time, generations
like towers, moated and alone,
nothing connecting the two except sight,
nothing passing but an occasional word.

One knows not to question such things:
the workings of miracles, the appearance
of strange plumed birds that fly
through one's pages or a young swan
landing in one's park in Belgium —
one knows not to question. Still
you remain so mysterious, so intense,
the air becomes electric and the flowers
frozen on their stems threaten to explode
as you pass. I hope you never change.

The Door

The door before me sits closed, dwarfish
and suggestive, and badly worn, an Italian
door in Cibiana, the Alps surrounding.
I imagine the owners leaving, closing this
for the last time, drawn into the order of things,
a threshold passed, as I sit waiting, the sun
slipping over the ridge. Just a little longer,
I whisper to my silent friend, *aspett' ancora*.

An hour ago, as I sipped my sweet bianco,
a sparrow landed on the balcony, curious
as he should be, pecking at unseen bits
upon the stair, his staggered movement
like that of an ancient chorus or tractor
on the hillside making its slow laps
across the slope and the inland gulls
squawking as they follow, a grand ballet.

This antique door, a gateway placed
just here above the barn, a balcony
trellised with painted flowers curling
even so, soundless in this abandoned
portico, overlooking the empty piazza,
yet the door holds out hope, a promise
as though a threshold into the future.
For this sad door I'll wait a while before
abandoning it once again to the darkness.

Night Thoughts on Athos

From my balcony I watch the darkening sky,
the sea at a distance blanketed by cloud,
and the crags below us like angry hands
reach towards heaven in quiet contemplation.
At Saint Anna's, the minor skete, life goes on,
the monks counting their private prayers,
knotted cords rubbed smooth by ancient hands.
This morning we sat drinking raki, saluting
our Russian friends, their skete a day's journey
north, the bare floor buffetted by the bootsoles
of pilgrims trekking through time and space
toward some undefined state of sublimity.
The rituals tonight would be no different,
the monks returning to their repast and wine,
to sit in the shadows remembering perhaps
the taverns of their youth — old friends, lovers —
abandoned to their solitude and thought,
the lights of ships traversing the near distance
tracing the ancient patterns, a few on the quay,
laden with cargo, the give and take of trade,
like prayer, as now in this meditative silence,
a spell only to be broken by the semantron,
its plaintive, wooden call to midnight offices,
novices standing round the lectern chanting,
fresh rain replenishing an ancient well,
and the old monks smiling as they remember,
climbing to their lofts, passing the icons,
censors smoking above the golden altars
and early elders lining the fissured walls,
towards which the brothers turn, returning
to dreams thrown out like nets across the sea,
retracing the mystic paths that brought them.
Looking down at the trail, it seems like years
since we arrived, welcomed by the brothers
busy at their craft, all illumined now by stars.
Perhaps this is what is meant by solitude,
the complicity of the hesychist calm, thoughts
that ripple on the surface of consciousness,
waves like soft breathing in the cultured, quiet air.

The Artist's Death

There's a man standing outside the half-
closed door of the dead youth —
a stranger, but he must have known
the boy, half again his age,
if one can guess such things. Perhaps
the two were friends, or tutor
and student. There is no expression
that would betray the answer.
Not grief, no, it's not grief one sees;
perhaps a certain contentment
that comes with the knowledge that something
is finally over; maybe that's
what there is to see in his face.
Outside the holiday continues,
the end of another year, the crowd swarming
noisily past, and yet not even this
seems to shake the man from his post;
but now he turns and moves off
once again into the street and the night
without a word, without a sigh.
In the dim light the artist rests
as though asleep, to wake
to his work, creating the world anew.
Outside the noisy celebration continues
without hope, without joy.

Road Adagio

*Tempus erat quo prima quies mortalibus aegris incipit
et dono divum gratissima serpit.*
--Vergil, Aeneid II.268-69

One recognizes something along the road
sometimes, telephone wires in fog
traced across the neon highway,
small hotels and street signs
punctuated by boredom hanging
on the horizon, a chord struck on clouds
to the accompaniment of the moon.

Somewhere along the way we spoke
of Berlioz, whispering conspirators,
like rebels invoking a new premise,
boasting fresh paradigms, of Brahms
entranced, notes open, composing
his eighteenth variation, in solitude.

Another night perhaps we'll speak
of Liszt and his heroes, shadows
of our first sleep, hushed nomads who ride
through our dreams, crossing boundaries
there where the stars come unexpectedly
together and only the memory
of a voice remains along the road.

Woman with a String

Hands poised to pull the mystery
taut, eyes burning
                    naked from the canvas,
the windows make one sense the present, the dream
lovers build between themselves.

I run my fingers over the canvas, the soft
red flame rising,
my fingers combing through the fire, and still
the eyes devour me.

It's the detail I remember, the shadow
thrown by the window one opens
through vision, and

I am pulled from both sides, past and future:
primitive echoes, sleeping and waking —
we structure both.

Last night I dreamt of elephants, native dancers
and windows, right and left,
the woman with string challenging me
to break the shell, alter and fly — yes, fly.

III.

The Barrette

The woman in front of me wears a barrette,
and I realize how easily I'm distracted
from the poetry being read only meters
away, burnished silver and copper buff,
a floral motif, accents of swirling brass,
its worked surface a studied landscape
where one could lose oneself, safe
and calm, and I imagine a poet there
relaxing in his art, hiding unobserved
till now in the young woman's hair,
looking back at me, perplexed by my gaze
scowling, perhaps, waving his arms
to distract me from watching his craft,
and I hear the speaker reading faster
to make his deadline, and I try frantically
to find my imagined friend again,
but she has shifted her head in anticipation
of departure, and he finishes his reading,
the applause begins, and she rises;
the moment vanishes, the silence returns.

Hokkaido in the 50's

The frigid river is still there, as before,
running through the town of my childhood,
the women along its banks hammering
their clothes upon the rocks, the market
further along and the sumo ring, its circle
under the thatched awning and the waiting
crowd, the echoing slap of their thighs,
just past the public baths and empty fields,
the rice pushing up as always despite the war.
The air was thick then with smoke, rising
from the huts, the sliding rice-papered doors
welcoming, inside the ancestral dolls
on cascading tiers of royal rubescent silk,
the early rulers, the ancient cortesans
in their flowing robes, mythic kings,
memories of a race slipping into the folds
of time, shuttles upon the weave of history.
The snow piled then as now pagoda-like
along the road, kids holding kimonos
high, the boys making their dutiful way
to practice, their *judogi* tied just so,
the bicycles and rickshaws passing by,
bowing to elders in their masks, laughing
joyously celebrating the day, Hotei
would not have surprised them as they walked
the traces, conjuring the *kami* spirits
imagined now from photos, the young standing
agape once again at the puppet show,
as we ski past in memory heading home.

Gallery Space

There are places one returns only in imagination
or rarely, or both, if one's lucky, places
where one feels the slight, soft press of one's hand
along walls and voices that trail from classes
long past, the primal portals of learning, harmonies,
like modern hieroglyphs carved into time;
behind some doors the mechanical whir of shredders
tearing up files, the random click-clack
of typists hidden in dark rooms, and on weekends
the young voices, a language you heard
long ago, and you smile listening to the children
just outside the gallery where you stand
once again there, hanging art and t-shirts, plastics
perhaps — where do these memories go?
Perhaps they are always here where we left them,
like a flower set on the sill of an old house
high in the mountains where you return years later
to find the flower still fresh, replaced
by some unknown hand, memories replenished
reworked by other imaginations, enjoyed
again and again, the poetry on the sill, in the gallery,
and we together once again in its grasp.

Bella Napoli

Eravate sublime/per cuore e accento/
il fuoco e il ghiaccio fusi
— Montale

A fusion, of darkness and light,
fire and ice, you sit beside the sea
contemplating paradise,
the sky disappearing, the sun dying.
How shall I imagine you —
light hair flowing beside you, rising,
arms outstretched, turning slowly,
palms out, fingers extended,
as though surrendering yourself
to the darkness and the sea.
And the darkness, as though called,
hits your hair, the moon your eyes,
and the sky fills with birds
always in pairs, rising in great circles
skyward, or lightning drifting
across the darkening, untrampled
sea floor, now silent,
only your figure remains bracketed
by the pulse of heaven.

Behind me the night teems
with quiet energy; the cadets returning
to their quarters, their scabbards clanking,
the sheathed steel now silenced.
We walk past the garden, the *teatro*
on our left, past the fountain,
on an uphill lane, a trattoria, a chance
discovery. Upstairs school kids
whisper in their local dialect
as they abandon us to the silence.
Now only the candle remains,
extinguished by the wind, its smoke
spiraling upwards into the dark,
the deep Neapolitan sky,
in this dream without a close,
sempre in questo sogno con te.

Game Day

Stony Lonesome, West Point

In the street the children play, bright
dresses, running and shouting, cool air
and trees, deer scampering with raised ear.
Somewhere a radio breaks the silence;
in the backyard the writer sits struggling,
his thoughts like worn unpruned roses.
Across the way a squirrel scampering
hoping for the peanut he's come to expect.
Unscored sheets, the autumn sun slanting
through the branches, the first hint of frost.
Leaves changing early, reds and golds;
next door the sitter rocks in her hammock
embracing her radio and her charge.
A bluejay swoops down spreading
its shadow beneath him on his canvas.
Two helicopters come into view, slicing
through the clouds, cadets standing ready
on the skids, seconds away from rappeling
through the flairs, long gray streamers,
and disappear down range over the treeline.
Then the quiet returns as the poet raises
his pen like a conductor's baton and begins.

Luca at Play

The young girl she once was sits quietly
before her Underwood for the first time,
slides in a sheet of paper, and begins:

clickity-clack the old typewriter sounds —
like a train going by, the bell and carriage
marking her progress — as she moves along

picking up speed and confidence, building
to full words, already feeling the power,
yet pausing to stare into the distance,

sensing a threshold to be crossed just here
before another line begins and thought
becomes phrasing, accumulating meaning,

as though waking from a dream, raising vague
fingers above keys as musicians might,
not knowing what to make of what she sees,

but knowing nonetheless that this is true,
that this is what she's meant someday to be,
where she will find a name, a voice, a life.

Gracie's Pulpit

Great Smokey Mountains

When Gracie was a girl, she climbed up here
thinking to touch the sky but touched
much more, and all the pain and all the years
that followed altered the verdant carpet
spread before her, caught as in a camera's flash,
imprinting the moment on her heart,
like hard cider, the rush, the promise, a place
from which she brought the voice of nature,
the green vast blanket of forest, the pulpit,

her marker, milestone ledge, legends
that spiral down the scree of memories,
lovers and loves past; just here she returns,
spreading her arms as though an army of dryads
were waiting, scattered across the valley,
their whispered sound rising and falling,
an Aeolian vesper to the evening sun
as it threads its way through the Needle's Eye,
and hemlocks dance to this melody on the wind.

Gracie knew the place well, the lodge
where they secluded themselves,
escaping protocol, stopping here
to mark their composure, their backdrop
majestic, rolling like a welcoming fog
that greeted them in the late winter snow
as unexpected as the passion neither
counted as real in their hilltop fantasy.

Today the hikers make their solitary way past
stopping a moment to catch their breath,
the timeless spectre of the woods below,
the faint trace of her scent, a lavender pressed
close in her diary marking the separate
moments of their union before he left
as many did for war, so unreal, the pulse
of their love and the eternal stillness,
an harmonic sounded then and no longer
as she hikes the trail in her dotage and lectures
the hemlocks on love and waste and time.

The animals pause as she goes, the trees sway,
and Gracie returns to her perch looking out
once again, as the sun lapses slowly
over LeComte's range and the four peaks
grow dim in the twilight and she closes
her eyes remembering — no tears, but resolve —
a secret held as the eagle might hold
its nest waiting for that faint inward clip, life
ending and beginning, and nature only a bit
altered continues on apace in the still,
damp throes of evening and then no more.

Girl Running

From my window I see a student running,
her backpack bulging as though she carried supplies
to wounded troops in the mountains
or were setting out upon some vernal pilgrimage
through forests, parsing her Latin sentences
to the light of a Coleman lantern;
in her hand she carries a ragged quire of pages,
perhaps a theme finished just at dawn, as the light
inched forward across her sill, dew forming
on the hyacinth along the path outside,
perhaps the long-awaited letter home
from a lover sitting on some distant desert cot,
a cloth to dry her brow, the sweat bleeding
through the headband, or his shirt left as rag
found in his drawer, behind old socks
the detritus of memory, as she rounds the curve,
disappearing finally from view, never guessing,
if ever our paths cross, why I smile
and thank her for her brief transit, an interlude,
the blink of a lens allowing her image
to leave its mark just before she vanishes.

Greek Dolls

The darkened shop sat below street level,
off Syntagma Square in old Athens;
from the sidewalk you see the center table,
the dolls, lying half composed, and the crones,
all in black, standing round, measuring out
cloth, crafting the drapes, embroidery,
the assignment of traditions and history.

Their ancient Karagouna beckoned me
into their twilight, finding upright bolts
of reds and blues, yellows, a vast array
propped against the walls, dark sepia photos
rough models for the half-created dolls.
Like cyclamen waiting their chance to bloom,
these dolls now sit above my desk, icons
calling me back into the streets of Greece
to hear again the lessons of the past,
to trace anew the music of my youth.

Hymettos

The hills have aged that once were strong,
sagging like the shoulders of ancient heroes
heavy with their rusting radar baggage.
Nearby in historic parks the statues stand
silent, devoured by a thousand suns,
and *koritsia* chasing their dreams of chastity
in the shade of plane trees blooming
from the temple base just off the garden trail.
Here on the Athens news our poet sleeps,
his lovers long in their earthen cradles,
and so his dreams. Here others daily plan
their new campaigns, the tourists misguided
with their empty smiles, sitting alone
in nearby *kafeneia*, wondering where
the classic form has gone, as the radars
make their sweep, sending drunken eyes
into the common void, this world where
gods have walked in times that are no more.

The Painter Going Blind

Here I'll place the black with the sound of fire
as it pours from the mouths of virgins,
black with their thoughts of summer,
and here the white shall marble
birds as they pass to the sea
already turned to stone, dull and silent.

Here gates shall stand unhinged for her return
from the pines where her lover waits,
the sprite bending to pick sweet alice
among thorns, her hair rippling
in white cascades, the slight give
as she moves through the trees,
and the sound that drives
the blood and brush in sympathy,
black as it runs down the leaf and is gone.

Here the canvas shall spread white
like fields of snow or sheets of autumn rain
blanketing the hills, and here —
just here — I'll paint her face in blacks
upon an endless sea of dreams.

Train Sounds at a Distance

Sometimes these sounds reach me at night,
a feeling like watching vapor trails and
hearing the jets pass softly and the silence
afterwards, as all the trains of my past
thunder by — flattening the penny offerings
we would leave on the track to appease the gods —
or like snow closing the distance between,
like mist spreading its drape, exploding
into a thousand pointillés, a veil sliding
from a remembered shoulder, that bends
to the flame of desire, or rain gentle
through the trees, and smoke billowing
from the hearth, quietly spreading
across the valley, the swirl of steam rising
from the café on the quay, the smell of coffee
as we watch the ships passing in the night,
their keels cutting into the unknown,
as the sound sweeps now across the field,
the husks absorbing the shock of the engine,
waves of sound sweeping out from its core
until the whisper attenuates to softness,
the faint whistle on the wind, and our dreams
turn elsewhere and the silence returns.

Little Johnnie, Auditor

Quiet, unmoving, little Johnnie sits watching
the ice cream truck slumber slowly past,
its ancient horse remarking him uneasily.
He blinks in the sun, and a moment of time
passes, the children coming to him slowly
as though whispering to an invisible friend
magically substantiated, timeless as the cracks
in the sidewalk or the old porch swing
that creaked under our combined weight, rocking
back and forth providing a rusty cadence call
to the invisible troop marching past on their way
west, and yes, I remember taking my place
beside him, inventing stories, creating worlds
for our friend John, wondering if we would
eventually learn what he seemed to know,
moving as we did into our own quiet solitude.

The Passing of Edward Schwarz

On the twelfth day before his coming death
he heard the drummer's sad tattoo, as though
for one yet unaware of what it means,
as for a sailor on the main, whose death

Were piped aloud across some ponderous bow,
a final passage, the cross of the mast
showing its bleached white sails to the night sky,
sailing into the darkness of his days,

And he remembered the farm of his youth,
the feed as it fell from his lording hands
and the hens as they dart about, scratching
the ground in unison, drumming the earth,

And his mother in her garden at dawn
dancing to music of the morning sun,
the others swaying to a melody
unheard by him, yet rising from the soil,

As they moved in the fragrant morning light
to their milking and churning, chores, and he,
too, helping to carry the floating curd —
all this he remembered as he lay dying.

He remembered also the forest pool
where he, the young boy, and the brutish swan
both claimed possession, each holding his sway,
a true image of still joy, boy and bird,

As memory expands and images fall
again into his vision, ducks and geese,
all nesting 'round his pool in the wood line,
his first spring rustling of warming desire,

And the rings that spread golden from its core
and his thoughts of women rising like sprites
from the mists, and he naked to the world's
dawn, saluting the morning sun, that day,

And then, too, an awareness of the end,
as on the fourth before his death he heard
these same birds calling him anew, water

cascading now across the fall of time:
The Normandy hens cackling in the brush,
and he, standing to strip himself at last,
diving again into the brackish deep —
all this he remembered as he lay dying —

The Columbines above them in the firs,
whispering to his young love beside the pool,
his first passion, nails digging into him,
neck and side, as the waves of their labors

Crest, and those three sweet hours of their travail
imprint a final image on his eye
at last; outside beyond his window's sill
a partridge on its morning branch takes wing

And rises light into the waiting sky.

The Arena

Verona, Italy

và, pensiero, sull'ali dorate

As the light dims, the libretto candles
explode as though a new firmament
were opening, sweeping across the stones,
illumination, the small books held
forward as though by a host of angels
attending word or song, a higher order.
Tonight, Nabucco, and we all await
the Hebrews' song echoing once again.
The evening before people sat in the rain
holding the last note heard, conjuring
the orchestra to sally forth from porticos
where they stood hidden, preserving
their instruments, but tonight the skies
are clear, two planes of mirroring stars.
A short walk east along the cobbled streets,
to Juliet's balcony and the Capulet house;
and north down Via Roma to the old castle,
whose bridge I cross each morning
greeting young lovers saying their goodbyes
as the river flows quietly below them
under bridges destroyed at war's end.
And now the orchestra arrives, tunes up,
salutes the audience, and begins.

The Myrtle Hour

Soft vespers toll the closing of the day
as the hour approaches, and you pass again
into my reverie, arriving now with fingers spread
like the eagle sent to awaken Cressida,
as the night moves forward towards the dawn
when all must begin again, leaving the dream,
and yet there you are rising in the darkness,
a spectre recalled as dying embers
remember the fire, my vague fingers
combing your raven hair, empty reflections,
empty shadows that crest just before waking
and your eyes look down at me, your spectral
body moving to the pulse we both can feel,
the rhythm slowing as day approaches,
until all fades into the dull amber of the day.

Summer Sketches

Bressanone, Italy

The mountain rises from the canvas, the blues
cascading over the mist-laden shoulders
of an oread awakened by chance, the sky
a drape falling slowly down her side,
like cloth in woodcuts from old carvers,
scented grass clinging still to their boots,
and she rises, barely visible, a brush mark
coming alive, paint blurring the near distance.

Over this airy expanse, our eyes catch now
the narrowing pathways, the early dew
running in rivulets, sun glancing off water
that rushes past in the cool morning,
the sylph escaping her bed, soft vestiges
of summer all rushing by in blues and oranges,
as the colors slowly soften, and we stand
surveying the miracle—the mountain, the sky,
the stream—opening, welcoming, ours.

Pictures in the Attic

The picture I wanted most to remember
has faded, the figures blurred.
One cannot tell how happy we were,
how we embraced
after the stranger snapped this picture, or that,
how we argued later and made love.
To see anything now requires an effort
of memory and imagination,
scattered moments bravely showing through.

I gather these old photos by handfuls —
dried flowers we expected to last forever,
moments of life, loose rectangles of hope —
holding them to the light, hoping still
to return the fire, restore the color.

It's the fading we didn't count on,
how the spirit slowly falls away
till nothing's left despite our efforts,
as though locking them away would save them,
as though this were answer enough

for such betrayals, why they leave us
and return, blurred images lost in time.

A Final Parting

Moments of farewell flow softly, gently by
like waves streaming round one's feet in wet sand.
Sitting alone here before reticulated stone,
I watch the light glinting along her sides, flanks
worked roughly smooth by these hands,
the cold marble silent, yet I imagine the heart
pulsing within, the eyes growing soft with time,
glimpsing in this quick moment the journey,
the dreams taking shape, the glyphs and curves
of her contours, her cool foot warming,
her back a canyon, the gentle river shimmering
slowly over pebbles rubbed smooth by time,
a bead of sweat making its languid, errant way,
memories carved into the awakening stone—
heat rising, a blush of pink marble, nothing more.

Notes

Cover photo: This photo I took on one of my frequent visits to the small Alpine town of Cibiana, whose ancient dwellings were saved from demolition by Italian artists who painted such beautiful murals on their walls that the historical center became one of the treasures of the region. I mention this town in "The Door."

"A Song for Miklós"
Miklós Radnóti, a teacher and poet, was born in Budapest to Jewish parents in 1909. He published a total of seven collections in his lifetime. He and his wife would eventually convert to Catholicism, but he was nonetheless drafted into forced labor because of his Jewish heritage. Working in the copper mines in Serbia, Radnóti and his fellow prisoners were force-marched in retreat as the Soviet forces approached. Weakened from hunger and torture, Radnóti collapsed and was shot. His body was dumped into a mass grave. When his body was exhumed a year later for proper burial, a small notebook of poems was found in his overcoat pocket. There is a statue to Radnóti in Hosok Memorial Park along the Danube in Mohacs, Hungary.

"Beyond the Statues"
George Seferis (1900-1971), a Greek poet and diplomat, won the Nobel prize in 1963.

"A Song for Melisande"
The poem is inspired by *Melisande,* a work by the Belgian painter Fernand Khnopff (1858-1921). The epigraph is from a poem, "Chanson de Melisande," by the Belgian poet Maurice Maeterlinck (1862-1949), Nobel laureate 1911. Although Maeterlinck was Flemish, he wrote in French. The passage may be roughly translated as "May the angels forgive us."

"Paraskevi"
The title of the poem can mean either Friday or preparation.

"Aurora"
The epigraph is from *Dämmerung* (Twilight, 1893), a play by Elsa Bernstein, an Austrian-German writer and dramatist of Jewish descent. The epigraph may be translated "the Twilight . . . one doesn't know its depth, but one feels it."

"Pizzica, the Spider's Dance"
The Pizzica is the name of a popular dance traditionally related to a rite of healing for the bite of a tarantula. *Masseria* is an Italian country house; *salice* is a red wine from the Puglia region.

"The Door"
See my note to the cover photo for Cibiana.

"Night Thoughts on Athos"
Mount Athos is the name commonly given to one of the peninsulae in the northern Aegean, now home to dozens of orthodox Greek and Russian monasteries and sketes, smaller annexes. The semantron mentioned in the poem is a percussion instrument of wood or metal used to summon the monks to prayer.

"Road Adagio"
The epigraph may be translated "it was the time when first sleep begins for poor mortals and creeps over them most pleasingly as a gift of the gods."

"Bella Napoli"
The epigraph is from "A Claudia Muzio" by Eugenio Montale (1896-1981), Nobel laureate 1975. The lines may be translated "you were sublime/in heart and accent/fire and ice fused."

"The Myrtle Hour"
According to European folklore if a young woman places a sprig of myrtle under her pillow on St. Catherine's Day, Nov. 25 (or alternatively on June 23, Midsummer's Eve), she will see her future husband in her dreams. The myrtle hour was usually at or right before midnight.

"The Chorus at Picasso's"
The epigraph is from "La Guitarra" by Federico Garcia Lorca (1898-1936). The lines may be translated "The weeping of the guitar begins. It is useless to silence it."

"Hokkaido in the 50's"
Judogi is the traditional name for the judo practice uniform. Kami spirits are those worshipped in the Shinto religion. Hotei is one of the seven gods of good fortune, associated with happiness and generosity, patron of children.

"Roping the Rhinoceros"
Bradamante is a female knight in Ludovico Ariosto's Orlando Furioso (1516).
.

Ted Higgs currently teaches Latin and Italian at Maryville College in Tennessee. He has taught at the college level for over 30 years—at the US Military Academy, the University of Maryland (European Division), Elizabethtown Community and Technical College, the University of Kentucky, and elsewhere—teaching language, literature, and creative writing. He is a retired Army officer and a linguist, having worked and translated in both Modern Greek and Italian. His poetry and translations have appeared in numerous journals. This is his first full-length book.

CPSIA information can be obtained
at www.ICGtesting.com
Printed in the USA
LVHW081755050819
626563LV00005B/118/P